DESTINY OF
LIGHT

Alan Hines

Order this book online at www.trafford.com
or email orders@trafford.com

Most Trafford titles are also available at major online book retailers.

Print information available on the last page.

ISBN: 978-1-6987-0801-0 (sc)
ISBN: 978-1-6987-0802-7 (hc)
ISBN: 978-1-6987-0800-3 (e)

Trafford rev. 06/18/2021

Trafford
PUBLISHING® www.trafford.com
North America & international
toll-free: 844-688-6899 (USA & Canada)
fax: 812 355 4082

BOOKS OF POETRY ALREADY PUBLISHED BY ALAN HINES,

1. Reflections of Love
2. Thug Poetry Volume 1
3. The Words I Spoke
4. Joyce
5. Constant Visions
6. Red Ink of Blood
7. Beauty of Love
8. Reflections of Love Volume 2
9. Reflections of Love Volume 3
10. True Love Poetry
11. Visionary.
12. Love Volume 1
13. This is Love
14. This Is Love Volume 2
15. This Is Love Volume 3
16. Garden of Love
17. Reflections of Love Volume 4
18. Reflections of Love Volume 5
19. Reflections of Love Volume 6
20. Reflections of Love Volume 7
21. Reflections of Love Volume 8
22. Reflections of Love Volume 9
23. Reflections of Love Volume 10
24. Godly Tendecies
25. Permanemt Blood Stain Volume 1
26. Permanemt Blood Stain Volume 2
27. Reflections of Love Volume 11
28. Lovely Joyce
29. Admiration of Love 3
30. Admiration of Love 4
31. Reflections of Love Volume 12 and Volume 13

URBAN NOVEL ALREADY PUBLISHED BY ALAN HINES,

1. Book Writer
2. Queen of Queens
3. Lost in a Poet Storm

UPCOMING BOOKS OF POETRY BY ALAN HINES,

1. Reflections of Love Volume 3
2. This is Love (Volume 1, 2, and 3)
3. Founded Love (Volume 1, 2, and 3)
4. True Love (Volume 1, 2, and 3)
5. Love (Endless Volumes)
6. Tormented Tears (Volume 1, 2, and 3)
7. A Inner Soul That Cried (Volume 1, 2, and 3)
8. Visionary (Endless Volumes)
9. A Seed That Grew (Volume 1, 2, and, 3)
10. The Words I Spoke (Volume 2, and 3)
11. Scriptures (Volume 1, 2, and 3)
12. Revelations (volume 1, 2, and 3)
13. Destiny (Volume 1, 2, and 3)
14. Trials and Tribulations (Volume 1, 2, and 3)
15. IMMORTALITY (Volume 1,2, and 3)
16. My Low Spoken Words (Volume 1, 2, and 3)
17. Beauty Within (Volume 1, 2, and 3)
18. Red Ink of Blood (Volume 1, 2, and 3)
19. Destiny of Light (Jean Hines) (Volume 1, 2, and 3)
20. Deep Within (Volume 1, 2, and 3)
21. Literature (Volume 1, 2, and 3)
22. Silent Mind (Volume 1, 2, and 3)
23. Amor (Volume 1, 2, and 3)
24. Joyce (Volume 1, 2, and 3)
25. Lovely Joyce (Volume 1, 2, and 3)
26. Pink Lady (Volume 1, 2, and 3)
27. Mockingbird Lady (Volume 1, 2, and 3)
28. Godly tendicies (Volume 1, 2, and 3)
29. Enchanting Arrays (Volume 1, 2, and 3)
30. Harmony (Volume 1, 2, and 3)

31. Realism (Volume 1, 2, and 3)
32. Manifested Deep Thoughts (Volume 1, 2, and 3)
33. Poectic Lines of Scrimage (Volume 1, 2, and 3)
34. Garden of Love (Volume 1, 2, and 3)
35. Reflection In The Mirror. (Volume 1, 2, and 3)

UPCOMING NON-FICTION BOOKS BY ALAN HINES,

1. Time Versus Life
2. Timeless Jewels
3. The Essence of Time
4. Memoirs of My Life
5. In my Eyes To See
6. A Prisoner's Black History

UPCOMING URBAN NOVELS BY ALAN HINES,

1. Black Kings
2. Playerlistic
3. The Police
4. Scandalous Scandal
5. The West Side Rapist
6. Shattered Dreams
7. She Wrote Murder
8. Black Fonz
9. A Slow Form of Suicide
10. No Motherfucking Love
11. War Stories
12. Race against time
13. Ghetto Heros
14. Boss Pimps
15. Adolescents
16. In The Hearts of Men
17. Story Teller
18. Kidnapping
19. Mob Ties

1. Her Soul To Take

As she lay down, down to sleep I pray the Lord her soul to take.
On earth she respresented you each day.
She said to see you in Heaven she couldn't wait.
To see the pearly gates.
To be amongst Christ, and his father each day.
The scriptures she dreamed of, and she'd read while awake.
A lovely lady that shined like the months of June, and May.
Behind the backs of others had nothing but good to say.
A memory that could never fade.
I pray, I pray the Lord her soul to take.

2. MY MOTHER'S MOTHER

My mother's, mother, grandmother.
I love you, it'll be no other.
Took things slow when it came to Satan she'd burn rubber.
Told me each man and woman are children of
God we're all sisters and brothers.
She told me to always reach for the skies go futher.
Keep hatred out your heart love, be a lover.
In the bible it says honor your mother and father,
and all God's children as sisters and brothers.

Grandmother I love, their could be no other.

3. ALL GOOD THINGS

Brought all good things to life.
Darkness to light.
The love of life.
I'f ever married I'd desire
someone like you as my wife.
What wonderful joy you brought to my life.
Fed me courage, wisdom, and insight.
Wish I had special powers to give
you second life.
Rest in Heaven,Eden,Paradise.

4. POSITIVE AND PRAY

Always look to see a brighter day.
Wash away negativity allow positive to stay.
Always remember the sun shine after rainy days.
Through it all bow down to the creator and pray.

5. FLY BUTTERFLY

Fly butterfly.
You came from being amongst
those that tried to walk over and stomp,
but you survived.
Was even considered an unattractive
caterpillar to the truth of naked eyes.
Through time you transformed to a beautiful
butterfly.
Spread your wings and shine,
fly, fly, high butterfly.
Let your beauty be an appealing
spectacle to the human eye.
Live soar above beyond,
the clouded skies.
Color, be as colorful as the brush
of the dead artist used when they were
alive. Let it be, be a way to believe,
to achieve, to give and blessings receive
in a magnificent kind.
Fly butterfly, fly high as a way of life.
A way of the transformation of progress within time.
Fly butterfly, fly forever so high.

6. SHINE

Ease minds.
Leave troubles behind.
Be divine.
Shine.
Allow each day to be happy like Valentine's.

7. LADY DREAM

A dream of what it seems.
I'm wishing for my fair lady to be
crowned as my queen.
A delightful human being.
Made of combinations of wonderful things.
A dream, a queen.
She brought the best out of everything.
My reality but seemed so great as a sweet dream.

8. MOTHER TIMES

Studied the clocks design.
Was always on time.
Did things appropriately on the right time.
Stayed ahead, never felt behind.
A divine mind stayed in church lines.
Against crime.
I miss sharing times.
Some say she was an angel
that was unleashed from God's mind.
Mother Hines.

9. Everlasting

I know you achieve everlasting life in Heaven.
But on Earth I wish you could've live forever.
When God took you away
I wish we could've died together.
For the love gave it'll get no better.

10. Pursuit

The power, pleasure, and pursuit,
of the kingdom within it reigns.
Happiness begins.
Free from sins.
Love within.
All are brothers, and sisters,
family and friends.
The pursuit, the chase of power,
and pleasure within,let the games begin....

11. 3526

3526 was your last place of residence.
You're always be loved, always be missed.
A womenly prince.
Truly Heaven sent.
Beautiful woman specimen.
Lived a life without sin.
Rest in paradise as for you it was meant.

12. Sweet Lady

Sweet lady lie to rest
in love is there in peace
I rest.
Love to death.
Spreaded love like no one else.

13. LOVE AND DIVINE

Lovely and divine.
The loveliest shine.
The best of her kind.
A divine creation of the creators
design.
Intelligent inquiring mind.
Loved all the time.
Lovely and divine.

14. LADY OF YEARS

Lady of all my years when I was a kid I'd
cry you'd whip away my tears, said in God's
heart I'd always live.
She told me even once she reach Heaven she'd still
be with me right here.
That the Lord is the only one I should fear.
Those that worship the Lord shall forever live eternal
life in Heaven is what it is.
In the church, and in the word, is where she lived.
My angelic lady of years.
I miss you momma, wish you was still here.
Lady of years.

15. GOD IS THE LIGHT

God is the light.
The kingdom of justice beyond sight.
Blessings giving baptism,
of new birth new life.
Visionary of sight.
The Creator of lovely days,
and peaceful sleep at night.

God is the light.

16. ROSE OF FLOWERS

Roses and flowers.
Praised God by the hour.
A sweet love that could never get sour.
Read the bible with power.

As beautiful as a Rose of a flower.

17. A Ribbon

I seen a ribbon in the sky.
It was my grandmother looking over
me from the skies.
I heard a voice say I love you without
any reasoning why.
Faithfully worship God on Earth
and will meet in Heaven once you die.
I see now your books of truth,
some of fictional,
scandals, and lies.
But keep writing to open up eyes,
strive for success until your coffen
coincides with your demise.
Forget what others may say
about your grind.
Keep doing what you do
write and leave your pass behind.
I love you son and see you in Heaven
somewhere down the line.
God bless you all the time.

18. FOR SO LONG

For so long,
the love was formulated built strong.
Carry on.
Arouse now growed up grown.
King James version,
a house, a home built of stone.

19. In Times Of

In times of need,
love indeed.
Unpolluted air to breathe.
A land filled of love,
of lovely deeds.

20. THE BIRDS

The chirping birds.
The church chorus sings melodies
of gospels words.
Love gave, deserved.
The spreaded wings of love,
of time, of lovely white birds.

21. GRACE AND TIME

Grace.
Love instead, not just case.

Time.
Time of love to never be defaced.

Pray.
Pray each day for the giving of living existing to
without dismay.

22. HAVE FAITH

Have faith.
Never go astray.
God is good,
God is great.

23. LOVELY AS THE

Lovely as the sunny days of sunshine.
Lovely as large red roses of hearts of Valentines.
Lovely as an angel of life, living breezing through times.
Lovely as the pleasure of being all mines.

24. THE REASON WHY I

The reason why I live.
The love you gave, give.
Blessed throughout seasonal greetings of years.

The reason why I live.

25. LIGHT OF MINES

Divine.
Shine.
This light of mines,
and I'm going to let it shine,
let it shine.
This little light of mines.

26. HIGHEST POWER

Highest degree.
Love to be.

Highest power.
Love to stand as a tour.

Highest love throughout
the seconds, minutes, and hours.

27. MY MOTHER'S MOTHER

My mother's mother.
A love like no other.

A reflection of God,
as my grandmother.

A profound woman,
love in abundance.

28. THE BEST

The best.
Loved that was deep through
your Earthly flesh.

Love to share the scriptures of God
to confess.

The best.

29. LADY OF TIMES

Lady of times.
Lady of spiritual rhymes.
Lady that was holy and divine.
Lady of love, light, shine.

Lady of times.

30. THE

The days, the nights.
A visionary of sight.

The progress of guidance,
the will the might.

The time frame,
the loyalty to God to remain.

31. MY LIGHT OF

My light of day.
Lovely one shine my way.

My light of mine.
Forever shine.

My light of love.
Heavens up above.

32. LOVE ENLARGE

The love of life,
the love of God.

The love living in which
made spiritual guidance enlarge.

33. SOUL TO UPRISE

In eyes.
Love lies.
Family ties.
Soul to uprise.

34. ELEGANT

My lady of love.

My lady of elegant touch.

My lady of shine in time to trust.

35. LOVE YOU EVER

Love you ever.
The greatest love ever.
Divine queen of God's cloth of an
angel's feather.

36. YOU ARE

Love who you are.
Shine like a star.
Be authentic be who you be,
who you are.

37. LOVE ALL DAY

Love all day.
Love everyday.
Love in a special way.

38. MY

My diamond, my pearl.
My lovely lady, my world.

39. LOVE THAT

In love.
Love that floods.
Addicted there of.
Addicted to your love.

40. THE EARS

The light.
The shine.
The love.
The grind.
The wisdom.
The ears to listen.

41. GOOD MOTHER

Good Mother.
Followed God in order to go futher.
A great woman.
Lovely grandmother.

42. SAVED

The life was gave.
Sanctified save.
Always prayed for better days.

43. THE PLEASANT SMELL

The pleasant smell of time.
Loved all the time.
Moved forward, no rewind.
Spiritually inclined.
Divine.

The pleasant smell of time.

44. RUG

Love.
High above.
Fly as Genie on a rug.

45. HEAVEN GAINED

Substain.
Love released from being contained.
Heaven gained.

46. NEW, SIGHT

Sight.
Delight.
New life.

47. ANGEL OF LOVE

Everlasting love.
Was love.
My angel of love.
Watch over me from Heaven's above.

48. AMPLIFIED LOVE

Amplified.
Love alive.
To forever live, alive.
Love to rely.

49. The Course Of

The course of the right track to stay focus.
Love as an anthem in which she wrote it.
Prayed daily afloat, speaking in tongue
catching the Holy Ghost.

50. TO BE ME

To be free.
To be me.
Lovely as a bird's nest in the trees,
lovely she.

51. LOVE MOUND

Love mound.
Love round and round.
Love by the pounds.
Love around.

52. SUMMER'S RAIN

Summer's rain.
Glorify her name.
Such a great dame.

53. LIGHT OF DESTINY

Destiny.
Heavenly.
Pleasantly.

54. SHARE MY LOVE

Share my love, never leave.
Together do good deeds.
Unpolluted air to breathe.
Love indeed.

55. IN THE SUNSHINE

In the sunshine forever more be mines.
Be my shine.
My Valentine.
My love of life to shine.

56. I WRITE

I sit write with my pen pouring out my
heart to you, my lover my friend.
My love for you has no end.
Thanks for the love as I was trapped in
the beally of the beast within.
My lover my friend, love as a perfected blend.
I love you again, and again.
My poetry and love letters to you
are heartfelt wrote in red ink of a pen.
My music for you be of love purified
with no sin.

57. CLOSER

Closer.
Holding me close.
Love's overdose.

58. ANGELIC LAYER

The magic we share.
Love always there.
Love as angelic layer.
The love, the magic we share.

59. Sweet Lady From Above

Sweet love.
Sweet lady from up above.
Thanks for the love.
Thanks for showing me what love is,
and was.

Sweet Love.
Sweet lady from above.

60. ONLY ONE

You're the only one for me.
The only one I can see.
Set my heart and mind free.

61. LOVE LESSON.

Love you got it and yes I can stand it.
Love is a lesson.
Love is a blessing.

62. ONE LOVE

Love me better.
One love you forever.
Pleasure.

63. Blessing of God

Receive the blessing of God.
Lovely as a shining star.
You are missed and love thus far.

64. ABOVE ME

Care.
Love me.
Put no one above me.

65. LOVE UTMOST

Love utmost.
Love the most.
Love to smoothly coast.

66. CROSSED MY MIND

You crossed my mind,
my lovely shine.
Lovely and divine.
I remember when I was left behind you came
to visit me, wrote letters to ease my mind.

You crossed me mind the love you gave
shall be in my heart a lifetime.

You crossed my mind took me back in time,
were love and happiness combined.
You be what the scriptures convey to
be holy and divine.

You crossed my mind,
although you're an ex,
I love you all the time.

67. READY

Ready for the world.
My Diamond, my Pearl.
Lovely as the rehab of third worlds.
My best lady, favorite girl.

Ready, ready for the world.

68. HER AND ME

You, and me.
You, and I.
As one until perishing tides.

69. RIBBONS

Ribbon of love.
Ribbon in the sky.
Ribbon of shoe laces to tie.
Ribbon in the sky of love
as being spiritually inclined
as the reason why.

70. I Need You

I love you.
I want you.
I need you.

71. REMEMBRANCE

When I was a kid you'd pick me up
and plant kisses, and give hugs,
always showed love.
Told me no matter what show love.
Each day pray to God above.
Let peace be multiplied, and show love.

My grandmother she was.

72. A Peak

Reach a peak.
Watch over me as I sleep.
I pray my Lord my soul to keep.

73. ALOT

Love alot.
Love non-stop.
Love by the flocks.

74. YOUR WINGS

To be free.
Lovely she.
Lovely lady spread your wings as an
angel to be free.

75. BETTER LOVE

To love.
Of love.
She was love.
I never knew a better love.

76. The Caress

Tender caress.
Love the best.
Love I confess.

77. MIDST

In the midst of time.
Made love to my mind.
Divine.
The best of her kind.
Another she I could never find.
Seem to be from the past,
that of another time.

78. Devoted to Serve

Devoted to serving God.
No matter what she was going through
she'd faithfully worship God.
Life always seemed easy instead of hard.
Had to be from another planet,
Saturn, Jupiter, Mars.
Shined like a star.

Devoted to serving God,
as her soul ignited love as firely spark.

79. GRIP

A love.
A lovely lady.

A time.
A time to ease minds.

A grip.
A grip as a cruise ship.

80. FEEL

The way she made me feel.
The superwoman of steel.

The way she made me shine,
proud to have you as mines.

81. MADE, GAVE

Gave.
Made.
Freed love in the coming of days.
Made it through a maze.
Loved in everyway.

82. TEST

The test of time.
Love all the time.
Love in mind.

83. IN WHITE

Lovely lady in white.
As the burning of time,
you planted seeds a great
premonition for the future to shine.
Treated people with love each time.
To her God was all she needed to breeze
through time.

84. Love She Be

Love she be.
Love you, and me.
Love as a visionary to see.

85. PATH

Stay on the right path, focus.
Continue living coasting.
Know that it's always good spirits
around, Holy Ghost.

86. TOUR GUIDE

To live.
Alive.
Tour guide of a pleasure ride.

Previously Published
Poems by Alan Hines:

LOVELY JOYCE

1. RAISED

Above and beyond raised.
Love that was genuinely gave.
Descendants that gave birth to lives was made.
Never left us alone,
always had a place to stay.
Loving, and missing you more,
and more each day.
Memories shall never fade.
The love you gave, in
paradise your soul was raised.

2. LEGACY OF LIVING

Life that was giving.
A lovely mother,
lovely children.
What a wonderful feeling.
To be loved, to be living.
Through seeded children,
you shall always be loved,
legacy of living.

3. FLY TIL THE END

Fly til the end of time.
We all living to die.
Enjoy the happiness,
sometimes pain will come tears to cry.
Through it all we gotta stay strong,
and give life a try.

Fly til the end of time.

4. ABOVE THE SKY

Mom, it seems as if I can see you above the clouds
in the sky.
Mom guess what, I sign more contracts,
books of poetry, and one of non-fiction of truthfulness
no lie.
When I'm home alone I shed tears of why.
Around your kids, and grandkids you know
I shall never ever let them see me cry.
Things aren't and will never be the same,
casket never wanted to see the inside.
Just wish you were still at home so I could stop by.
In peace in the Haevens wings to fly,
fly mom high above the sky.

5. Ruler Of My World

I see your reflection in waters of midnight lakes
within this world.
My diamond my pearl.
Birthed me, made it warmful in this cold world.
Could see your face would always be present in
times of despair, turmoil.
Times of less, made it happen, blessed,
a continious swirl.
Loved your seeds shared your world,
a crown, a ruler,
she ruled the world.

6. YOU

A representation of you.
A reflection of you.
Everything I have is because of you.
My lady hero, my love unto.
My love overwhelmed as always due.
The trueness of true.
My lady above the skies,
my lady sky blue, you.

7. BELIEVE IN LOVE

Believe in love,
believe in light.
God will shine his light.
An awakening in paradise.

8. MEMORABLE MEMORIES

Memorable memories.
In my slumbers, and visions is all I see.
From birth, your first seed.
The last of a dying breed.
Once Earthly lady enjoy yourself
being Heavenly freed.
Indeed memories never cease to proceed.
Love to be, as I'll make you proud
of me.
Melodies harmony, memories.

9. Feeling It

I'm feeling it from my head to my toes.
Feeling it never wanted to let go.
Feeling it mom I love you so.

10. RISING IN THE SUN

Rising in the sun.
As birth become, begotten son.
Made my childhood lovely and fun.
Honored to be thou son.
Distinguished woman my numero uno, my number one.
I see reflections of you through the lake shores,
that glistens your smile through the rising of the sun.
An angelic angel you arouse to paradise to become.
Shine forever, out shine the rising of the sun.

11. PREVAIL

Ringing of bells.
Wish you well.
Fly high prevail.

12. I Can't Believe

I can't believe this
day finally become.
Wish you could've lived in the form
of flesh,
forever more to come.
Peace atleast, sleep tight mom.

13. My Lovely Queen

She had me when she was only sixteen.
A lovely young lady a beauty queen.
Love me more than things really seemed.
Been there through it all when
low income dried up streams.
The woman that gave me life to dream.
Upon judgement day you shall
inherit eternal life,
meet the king of kings.
My lovely lady my beauty queen.

14. NEVER WANTED TO SEE

Never wanted to see you leave.
Not in front of the audience,
but in my heart, mind, soul, I shall forever
grieve.
Your life gave me life nourishment to feed.
If you had it I was never in need.
My lovely lady forever to be.
My love, my lovely lady Joyce
I never wanted to see you leave.
My whole hearted love shall forever bleed.

15. MEMORY LANE

In loving memory, I remember
almost everything as I float down memory lane.

I remember as a kid in snowy winter times
of Christmas you made it rain.
Wish I could hear your voice again.
I just love hearing your name.
It is a shame,
but Heaven gain.

16. SWEET DREAMS

A shining sensational delight.
Gave me hope, shining lights, gave me this life.
Reached great heights.
Peacefully sleep, sweet dreams
throughout the dreams and nights.

17. Precious Lady

Precious lady.
Precious lady of living.
So wonderful, so forgiving.
Reach out to those in the projects
as if they was your own children.
Precious lady of giving.

18. MOTHERLY LOVE CAST ANGELS

Motherly love cast angels from up above
be a guardian angel for those drowning
in floods.
Feed the hunger with food of love.
Be a shield from violence, a rehab for drugs.
Motherly love cast angels from up above
be our savior, savior of love.

19. 2515 W. JACKSON

2515 W. Jackson.
Overlapping, relapsing heart
collapsing, love everlasting.
Back to the past missing you like action.
2515 W. Jackson.

20. CUTE

She was cute in her eternal sleep,
but she looked better when she was alive
arouse I wish I pray I hope love floats.

21. Thanks To You

Thanks to you I write music for artist to sing
also poetry is my thing.
On Earth you gave birth to me as your
first born seeded king.
As a teenager you provided me with this
life to live live out my dreams.
To me you mean more than the world my angel
my motherly queen.
Rest in Heaven sleep tight
and sweet dreams.

22. GOOD HEART

Good heart.
Love never depart.
Offspring she'd never be apart;
would travel to the depths as astronauts far.
Loved genuinely accepting people through their flaws
of who they really are.
A marvelous star.

23. LOVELY MOTHER

Lovely mother,
they'll never be no other,
not another.
Blessed to be your son,
blessed to be able to go futher.

24. BIRTH

White birds that fly from the palms
of my hand to the sky,
wishing this day had never become.
Love you, and miss you mom.
You from birth in which I come from.
Loving in sums,
praying and reading Psalms.
To the east I face, to the skies up my palms.
Memorable visions shall never fade, as since birth
they begun.

25. Best Of You

As you were, as you'll forever be,
memories.
You gave the best of you, wanted a better me.
Wanted me to forever be free.
Wanted me to get out live a little,
sights to see.
Said I'd make a good husband to my wife
when I decided to marry.
Poetry being read as my fingers caress
the piano's keys, sweet melodies.
Best it ever was, gave the best of you to me.

Printed in the United States
by Baker & Taylor Publisher Services